A POCKET GUIDE FOR GOLFERS

RICK GRAVES
TERRY GLASPEY

HARVEST HOUSE PUBLISHERS
EUGENE, OREGON

Cover photo © Chris Garborg / Garborg Design Works, Savage, Minnesota

Cover design by Garborg Design Works, Savage, Minnesota

A POCKET GUIDE FOR GOLFERS
Formerly *The Hackers Almanac* and
52 Amazingly Simple Secrets for Better Golf

Copyright © 2006/2007/2011 by Terry Glaspey and Rick Graves
Published 2011 by Harvest House Publishers
Eugene, Oregon 97402
www.harvesthousepublishers.com

ISBN 978-0-7369-3732-0

Printed in the United States of America

11 12 13 14 15 16 17 18 19 / BP-SK / 10 9 8 7 6 5 4 3 2 1

INTRODUCTION

If you love golf, this pocket guide is for you! This collection of amazingly simple but extremely effective tips for improving your score; jokes and tongue-in-cheek humor about the game; interesting facts, history, and trivia; and insightful quotes about this wonderful and sometimes infuriating pastime called golf will entertain and teach you for hours. Rick Graves is a former teaching professional who knows a thing or two about golf. Terry is a golf fanatic who knows he needs to hold on to his day job and celebrates the advice once offered by G.K. Chesterton: "If a thing is worth doing, it's worth doing badly."

Whatever your skill level—absolute beginner, longtime hacker in search of improvement, or skilled golfer—you'll find something helpful and enjoyable in this book.

The concluding section of this book contains 101 practical, easy-to-digest tips on nearly every aspect of the game. These tips are not complicated or confusing.

We call them "amazingly simple" because they are just that. Rick distills foundational basics into understandable and easy-to-follow-steps that will help you improve your game. People tend to make things too complicated. Anyone who has spent time studying the mountains of golf instruction books knows it is easy to be overwhelmed and confused by all the advice the experts offer. Perhaps you've stood over a putt with your mind spinning with dozens of "suggestions" about stance, grip, pace, and other factors in making a good stroke. Hard to make a good run at it with all that going on in your head. But if you pay attention to Rick's amazingly simple tips, you are sure to shave a few strokes off your score!

A Pocket Guide for Golfers also reveals the history and traditions of this great game and the outstanding achievements of the greatest golfers of all time. We hope you'll smile—and even laugh out loud—at the humorous observations by and about golfers and the strange ways people pursue the passion of chasing a little white ball across the green grass. So tuck this little book into your golf bag or carry it with you for those spare minutes that pop up occasionally and then dip into it for some inspiration!

Rick Graves
Terry Glaspey

Golf is a great game because it allows one
to run the gamut of emotions in a
four-hour span without harming anyone.

BOB JONES

10 REASONS WHY GOLF
IS BETTER THAN BOWLING

1. You don't have to wear someone else's shoes.

2. The shirts are infinitely more fashionable.

3. You get three or four hours away from home rather than 45 minutes.

4. You can't hit your bowling ball out of the gutter.

5. No one ever broke his toe by dropping a golf ball on it.

6. The scenery never changes at the bowling alley.

7. You get lots of fresh air out on the golf course; the bowling alley smells like sweaty socks.

8. In bowling, your score is flashed up on the screen for everyone to see.

9. How many great bowling stories have you heard over the years?

10. In golf, someone comes around in a cart and offers you refreshments. In bowling, the guy handing out the shoes also serves you nachos.

10 TIPS FOR BETTER PUTTING

1. Never rush a short putt.

2. On short putts, *listen*—don't look—for the ball to go in.

3. Pick a line and believe in it.

4. *Right-handed players:* On putts, address the ball just inside your left foot for a smoother roll. *Left-handed players:* On putts, address the ball just inside your right foot for a smoother roll.

5. Always accelerate through a putt.

6. Keep the putter head even with or behind your hands on short putts.

7. Leave yourself tap-in second putts. It saves wear and tear on the nerves.

8. Don't change putters. Find one you love and marry it.

9. Keep your knees very still during your stroke.

10. Think about the target, not about fundamentals, when putting on the course.

10 TIPS ON GOOD GOLF MANNERS

1. Never say "Knock it in" just as a player is ready to putt.

2. Keep out of a player's view as he plays a shot.

3. Stop talking to a player one minute before he is ready to play a shot.

4. Never yell "Good shot" until the ball has stopped rolling and has proven to be a good shot.

5. Don't give advice until someone asks for it.

6. Be ready to play when it's your turn.

7. Around the green, watch where you're walking and be ready to tend the flagstick if someone asks you.

8. Learn to count properly.

9. Announce your score after every hole so the scorekeeper doesn't have to ask.

10. When someone asks, "What did you shoot?" just say the number. Don't give a speech. The questioner doesn't care about your bad luck; he only wants to know if he beat you.

10 WARM-UP DRILLS

1. Hold your club horizontally against your back with both elbows around it. Bend slightly and make slow turns back and forth.

2. With your legs as straight as possible, bend at the waist and let your arms hang toward the ground for 15 to 30 seconds. Don't bounce. Repeat a few times.

3. Hold your club in front of you in one hand with your arm parallel to the ground and your club pointing skyward. Slowly rotate the club down to the ground to one side, back up, and then down to the ground on the other side. This loosens your forearm muscles and creates a more fluid swing.

4. Take a stance, turn your upper body toward your target, and bend at the waist, reaching both arms down so your fingers point toward the heel and toe of one shoe. Then stand up and turn the other way, reaching for the heel and toe of the other shoe. Repeat a few times.

5. Take three irons, hold them all by the grips, and make a number of slow swings. Do not swing fast or hard.

6. Lie on the ground and do a push-up from the waist up, leaving your belt buckle on the ground. Arch your back and hold. (This is known as the cobra position.) Let yourself down slowly and repeat a few times.

7. Holding onto something to steady yourself, grab a foot and pull it back so the heel reaches or nearly reaches the buttocks. Hold for 30 seconds and then stretch the other leg. Do three repetitions.

8. Hold your arms out in front of you and open both hands wide with palms down, stretching your fingers for 10 seconds. Drop your arms to your side. Wait 30 seconds and repeat. Do three repetitions.

9. Fold your arms, assume a golf stance, look at an imaginary ball, and slowly make backswing and forward swing motions, forcing one shoulder and then the other under your chin. Do ten repetitions.

10. If time does not allow for a thorough warm-up, make 20 continuous swings, easy at first, back and forth without stopping. Make sure to do this early so you have at least three minutes to rest before teeing off.

THE GREATEST GOLFERS OF ALL TIME

The 1800s
Tom Morris Jr. (Scotland)
Willie Park Sr. (Scotland)

1900–1920
Harry Vardon (England)
James Braid (Scotland)
Willie Anderson (Scotland)
Francis Ouimet (USA)
Jim Barnes (USA)

1921–1940
Walter Hagen (USA)
Gene Sarazen (USA)
Bobby Jones (USA)
Tommy Armour (USA)
Henry Cotton (England)
Ralph Guldahl (USA)
Byron Nelson (USA)

1941–1960
Sam Snead (USA)
Ben Hogan (USA)
Jimmy Demaret (USA)
Bobby Locke (South Africa)

Cary Middlecoff (USA)
Peter Thomson (Australia)

1961–1980

Arnold Palmer (USA)
Gary Player (South Africa)
Jack Nicklaus (USA)
Billy Casper (USA)
Lee Trevino (USA)
Tom Watson (USA)
Hale Irwin (USA)
Johnny Miller (USA)
Ray Floyd (USA)

1981–1995

Seve Ballesteros (Spain)
Greg Norman (Australia)
Nick Price (Zimbabwe)
Nick Faldo (England)
Bernhard Langer (Germany)
Payne Stewart (USA)

1996–Present

Tiger Woods (USA)
Ernie Els (South Africa)
Vijay Singh (Fiji)
Phil Mickelson (USA)
Padraig Harrington (Ireland)

9 BAD SHOTS:
THEIR CAUSES AND CURES

1. The shank

Hitting a portion of the ball on the hosel causes a lateral shot to the right.* To cure the shank, take the club straight back and up on the backswing. Come through with a slight outside-in path to eliminate the inside and laid-off backswing, which causes the misfire. (*Left-handed golfers: Substitute left for right and right for left when reading this list.)

2. The chili-dip

On short pitches and chips, hitting the shot "fat" leaves the ball embarrassingly close to you after impact with the turf. This is caused by playing the ball too much in the center of the stance and often by using other than a sand wedge, which has a bounce flange to prohibit chunking or chili-dipping. The cure is to play the ball off your back foot so you're more likely to contact the ball before the ground.

3. The banana ball

This is caused by an outside-in swing with little shoulder turn and no rotation of the forearm on the forward swing. The cure is a one-piece takeaway with plenty of shoulder turn against a braced right knee. On the forward swing, attempt to roll the toe of the club shut earlier in the swing. This cure is rarely attainable without the coaching of a PGA professional.

4. The snap hook

This is the reverse of the banana ball and is only a problem for a somewhat accomplished player. Among the multiple causes is an overactive right hand in the swing to compensate for bad balance and/or no leg drive. If it occurs during a round, squeezing hard with the right ring finger to inactivate the thumb and forefinger will increase the chances of properly driving the right elbow into the side rather than allowing it to fly out as the right hand causes the clubhead "hit" to occur before impact.

5. The pop-up drive

This infuriating shot is caused by too steep a takeaway rather than a nice low one. The cure is to keep slightly more weight on the back foot and start the takeaway with the shoulders and arms as a unit. Avoid a wristy, quick pickup.

6. The missed gimme putt

Aside from a misalignment problem, the most likely cause of a missed two-footer is a deceleration of the clubhead through impact or a folding left wrist through impact. This shot is a plague even for accomplished tour players, and no one knows when it will occur.

7. The skulled shot

This mishit usually happens when the player has not hit down enough on the shot, either through stiff knees, causing poor balance, or by "flinching" through the swing. The cure is to imagine a tee under the ball and aggressively attack down to clip the tee.

8. The unsuccessful bunker shot

Assuming your sand iron is engineered properly (see your pro to be sure), the most common reason your ball stays in the bunker is that you're simply not swinging hard enough. With a few inches of sand between the club and ball at impact, a 30-yard swing will propel the sand shot 30 feet. Don't let your instinct fool you. Swing harder than your eyes tell you to.

9. The whiff

Why do golfers sometimes miss the ball completely? The causes are too numerous to mention. See your pro or buy a bowling ball. As long as your fingers get out of the ball as you throw it, no bowling whiff will occur.

11 OF THE MOST COMMON PENALTIES

1. Hitting the ball into a water hazard

Penalty: one stroke. Replay the shot from the original spot or drop a ball directly behind the water hazard on a line from the flagstick through the point of entry. In a lateral hazard, a player has three options:

A. Drop a ball within two club lengths of the spot where the ball crossed the margin of the hazard. Drop on either side of the hazard but not nearer to the hole.

B. Replay the shot from the original spot.

C. On a line from the flagstick through the point of entry, play as far back as desired.

2. Lost ball

Penalty: one stroke. Replay the shot from the original spot. You can play a provisional ball before searching if you think your ball might be lost.

3. Hitting a ball out of bounds

Penalty: one stroke. Replay the shot from the original spot.

4. Grounding the club in a hazard

Penalty: two strokes or loss of the hole in match play.

5. More than 14 clubs in your bag

Penalty: two strokes for each hole (maximum of four strokes) or loss of hole in match play (maximum of two holes).

6. Hitting an unattended flagstick with a putt

Penalty: two strokes or loss of hole in match play.

7. Ball moves after address

Penalty: one stroke penalty. Replay from the original spot.

8. Ball moves while moving a loose impediment

Penalty: one stroke. Replay from the original spot.

9. Recording the wrong score on your scorecard

Penalty: if you sign a score lower than the actual score, you are disqualified. If you sign a score higher than the actual score, the higher score stands.

10. Unplayable lie

Penalty: one stroke. Drop a ball within two club lengths but not nearer to the hole. You can also go back as far as you want (on club property) and drop on a line extending from the flagstick through the point of unplayable lie.

11. Playing a wrong ball

Penalty: two strokes or loss of hole in match play.

5 MEMORABLE MASTERS

1. Six years after his last major championship victory, *Jack Nicklaus* trails by six strokes with ten holes to go and shoots a record-setting 30 on the back nine to win at age 46 (1986).

2. *Tiger Woods* wins his first major with a record-setting 270 and a 12-stroke margin of victory (1997). His 2001 triumph makes him the first golfer to hold all four major championship trophies at the same time.

3. Down three strokes with four holes to play, *Gene Sarazen* holes his second shot (a 4-wood) on the fifteenth hole and goes on to win in a playoff (1935).

4. In a three-man playoff, *Larry Mize* pitches his chip shot into the hole to defeat Greg Norman and Seve Ballesteros (1987).

5. *Arnold Palmer* birdies the final two holes to win his second green jacket (1960).

5 MEMORABLE PGA CHAMPIONSHIPS

1. Long-hitting unknown *John Daly* is a crowd-pleasing, fist-pumping winner at Crooked Stick (1991).

2. *Walter Hagen* wins the first of five PGA Championships in a match play victory over former champion Jim Barnes at Inwood Country Club (1921).

3. After consecutive bogeys and a badly sliced tee shot on the sixteenth hole, *Gary Player* seems to have lost any chance of winning at Oakland Hills. He can't see the flagstick and has to borrow a chair from someone in the gallery to line up his shot. It narrowly clears both trees and water and stops four feet from the hole. He sinks the putt for birdie and goes on to win with pars on the last two holes (1972).

4. One day before he is scheduled to report for duty in the U.S. Navy, *Sam Snead* defeats Jim Turnesa in match play for his first major championship victory (1942).

5. *Tiger Woods* follows up victories in the U.S. Open and British Open with a nail-biting victory over Bob May in a playoff duel at Valhalla (2000).

5 MEMORABLE U.S. OPENS

1. *Arnold Palmer*, seven strokes behind the leader going into the last round of the U.S. Open at Cherry Hills, decides his only chance for victory is to go for broke. He drives the green on the first hole, a 346-yard par 4. He birdies that hole and five of the next six. He finishes with 65 and the victory (1960).

2. On his way to a Grand Slam (at that time consisting of the U.S. and British Opens and the Amateur championships), *Bobby Jones* wins at Interlachen. It is the last year he plays competitively (1930).

3. The one-hundredth U.S. Open marks *Jack Nicklaus'* final appearance and *Tiger Woods'* record-setting performance at Pebble Beach en route to the "Tiger Slam" (2000).

4. *Payne Stewart* wins at Pinehurst, course 2, with an unforgettable 20-foot putt on the final hole (1999). America is stunned when he dies shortly after in a plane accident.

5. *Tom Watson* chips in en route to his victory at Pebble Beach (1982), robbing Jack Nicklaus of a fifth U.S. Open win.

5 MEMORABLE BRITISH OPENS

1. *Tom Watson* outduels Jack Nicklaus at Turnberry with a birdie on the seventeenth hole (1977).

2. *Tiger Woods* is victorious by eight strokes at St. Andrews to complete a career Grand Slam at only 24 years of age (2000).

3. Jean Van de Velde triple-bogeys the final hole at Carnoustie to set up a playoff. *Phil Laurie* wins after starting the day ten strokes back (1999).

4. *Bobby Jones* wins his last British major in Hoylake before retiring from tournament play (1930).

5. *Seve Ballesteros* wins an emotional victory at St. Andrews in a head-to-head last-round battle with Tom Watson (1984).

10 PIECES OF GOLF ADVICE
WE'RE TIRED OF HEARING

---

1. Watch how the pros do it.

2. Don't overthink the shot.

3. Buy a new driver.

4. Buy a new putter.

5. Visualize the ball going right down the middle of the fairway.

6. Aim for the flagstick.

7. Just relax and follow through.

8. Be the ball.

9. Don't think about the water hazard.

10. Just play one hole at a time.

10 GOLF RULES WE'D
LIKE TO SEE IMPLEMENTED

1. Anything inside 20 feet is considered a gimme.

2. Hitting a ball into a water hazard means an automatic mulligan.

3. If you can't break 100, you're not allowed to dispense advice to another golfer.

4. If it takes more than five minutes to find your ball in the rough, the shot never happened.

5. If your ball doesn't escape the sand trap on your first attempt, you're allowed to toss it onto the green.

6. If you can't break 100, you are not allowed to wear any clothing with a golf logo on it.

7. If your opponent takes more than two minutes to execute his shot, you are allowed one swing at him with the club of your choice.

8. If you can see the ball—regardless of where it is—it is considered a playable lie.

9. Any drive that hits a slow-playing golfer is considered an automatic birdie.

10. You cannot shoot higher than seven on any hole. After the seventh shot, just write it down, hang your head, and move on.

THE FOURSOMES WE'D LOVE TO SEE

All-Time Favorite Foursomes
Rick: Bob Hope, Arnold Palmer,
Ben Hogan, Rodney Dangerfield

Terry: Jack Nicklaus, Ben Hogan,
Arnold Palmer, Bobby Jones

Best Scramble Team of All Time
Tiger Woods (to hit tee shots)
Ben Hogan (for accurate iron shots)
Ray Floyd (for creative short game)
Jack Nicklaus (to sink the putts)

"Hardest to Concentrate on Golf" Foursome
Gerald Ford, Jack Lemmon,
Bill Murray, Chevy Chase

Most Volatile Scramble Team of All Time
Tommy Bolt, Tom Weiskopf,
Craig Stadler, John Daly

Calmest Scramble Team of All Time
Dave Marr, Tom Kite,
Ernie Els, Davis Love III

THE 6 SWEETEST SWINGS IN GOLF

Sam Snead

Gene Littler

Bobby Jones

Al Geiberger

Payne Stewart

Steve Elkington

A FEW TERMS EVERY
GOLFER SHOULD KNOW

---

ace: a hole in one

albatross: a double eagle, a three-under-par score on a hole

away: farthest from the hole and the first to play

beach: a sand trap

birdie: a one-under-par score on a hole

bite: enough backspin to keep the ball from traveling very far once it lands

bogey: a one-over-par score on a hole

bunker: a type of hazard, usually filled with sand

carry: the distance the ball travels in the air before it hits the ground

casual water: standing water or rain puddles that do not constitute a permanent water hazard and from which you are allowed to take relief

chili-dip: a chip shot in which the club hits the ground before the ball, resulting in a shot that only travels a few feet

choke: 1. collapse under pressure, 2. grip further down on the club handle than usual

dogleg: a hole with an angled fairway

double bogey: a two-over-par score on a hole

double eagle: a three-under-par score on a hole

draw: the flight of a ball that curves to the left because of sidespin (*left-handers:* ball curves to the right)

eagle: a two-under-par score on a hole

fade: the flight of a ball that curves to the right because of sidespin (*left-handers:* ball curves to the left)

flier: a shot that goes farther than normal

fried egg: a ball that is mostly buried in sand

frog hair: the grass surrounding the putting green, which is usually cut shorter than the fairway but taller than the green itself. Also called the *fringe.*

get legs: an encouragement for the ball to keep going

gimme: a putt that is so close your opponent doesn't require you to putt it out

green: the closely mown grass where the flag and hole are placed

hacker: a slang term for a poor golfer

hazard: a penalty area; an area that uses sand, water, or other obstruction to add challenge

honor: the privilege of teeing off first

hook: a mishit that has too much sidespin and ball curves dramatically to the left (*left-handers:* ball curves to the right)

kitty litter: a bunker filled with sand

knockdown shot: a shot that stays low in the wind

lip: the edge of the cup. A narrow miss that catches the edge of the cup is said to "lip out."

mulligan: a shot that is replayed without a penalty. Not allowed in official scoring and usually limited to the first hole.

nineteenth hole: the clubhouse, where players often meet after playing 18 holes

on the dance floor: on the green

pin: flagstick

pop-up: a shot that catches the top edge of the driver face, resulting in a high, ineffective trajectory

punch shot: a knockdown shot, a shot that stays low in the wind

relief: an improvement of your lie without a penalty

sandbagger: a player who sports a deliberately high handicap to win competitions

shank: a hit on the hosel of the club, resulting in an errant shot to the right (*left-handers:* ball goes to the left) *sit:* an encouragement for the ball to stop as quickly as possible

slice: a mishit that has too much sidespin and curves dramatically to the right (*left-handers:* ball curves to the left)

slope: a rating of the difficulty of a course

snowman: a score of eight on a hole

sweet spot: the ideal place on the clubhead to strike the ball for the best results

tap-in: a putt of two or three inches

tee: 1. the area from which the first shot of the hole is played, 2. a peg on which the ball is placed

triple bogey: a three-over-par score on a hole

trap: a slang name for a bunker

up and down: getting the ball in the hole in two strokes when starting from off the green

whiff: a swing that fails to make contact with the ball

worm burner: a shot that rolls along the ground instead of soaring through the air

yips: nervous tension that causes missed short putts

10 MOST ANNOYING
GUYS ON THE COURSE

---

1. The guy who takes five minutes to line up and measure every putt even though he never makes one outside of two feet.

2. The guy with the latest, most expensive driver.

3. The guy who gives you a golf lesson after every hole.

4. The guy who yells, "You da man!" even after you duck-hooked your drive 135 yards into the woods.

5. The guy who does the Tiger Woods fist pump after every putt he makes.

6. The guy who always asks about yardage.

7. The guy who insists on quoting from *Caddyshack* throughout the round.

8. The guy who attempts to bounce the ball on his pitching wedge.

9. The guy who never seems to be watching when you hit a great shot.

10. The guy who regales you with stories of his greatest shots though you've never seen him make one.

MOST CAREER WINS ON THE PGA TOUR

As of January 1, 2011

Sam Snead (82)	Lloyd Mangrum (36)
Jack Nicklaus (73)	Vijay Singh (34)
Tiger Woods (71)	Horton Smith (32)
Ben Hogan (64)	Harry Cooper (31)
Arnold Palmer (62)	Jimmy Demaret (31)
Byron Nelson (52)	Leo Diegel (30)
Billy Casper (51)	Gene Littler (29)
Walter Hagen (44)	Paul Runyan (29)
Cary Middlecoff (40)	Lee Trevino (29)
Gene Sarazen (39)	Henry Picard (26)
Tom Watson (39)	Tommy Armour (25)
Phil Mickelson (38)	Johnny Miller (25)

10 GREAT MOVIES ABOUT GOLF

Follow the Sun (1951)

Glenn Ford stars as Ben Hogan in an inspiring (if not always historically accurate) film about how Hogan survived a near-fatal car crash and returned to triumph as a U.S. Open champion. Contains cameos by Sam Snead, Cary Middlecoff, Jimmy Demaret. Many consider this the best movie ever made about professional golf.

Caddyshack (1980)

This comedy featuring Chevy Chase and Bill Murray may not be the best movie about golf, but it is one of the most popular. Some of it is a bit silly, but the best moments are hilarious and absolutely classic.

Tin Cup (1996)

Kevin Costner stars as a down-on-his-luck professional who has fallen to working at a decrepit driving range until he is challenged to work his way back into the game, ending up as a contender for the U.S. Open. Peter Jacobsen, Johnny Miller, Craig Stadler, and Gary McCord all provide entertaining cameo appearances.

The Legend of Bagger Vance (2000)

Based on the novel by Stephen Pressfield, this is the story of a disillusioned war veteran (played by Matt Damon) who learns the secret of the authentic golf swing from his mysterious caddy (played by Will Smith).

Happy Gilmore (1996)

Adam Sandler is an acquired taste, but there are definitely some good laughs (the best one involving Bob Barker) in this story of a frustrated hockey player who joins the pro tour because he can hit the ball 400 yards with his very unorthodox swing.

Pat and Mike (1952)

Tracy and Hepburn team up for a thoroughly entertaining story about a female golfer and her hard-nosed promoter. Cameos by Babe Zaharias, Betty Hicks, and other women's tour professionals add to the fun.

Bad Golf Made Easier (1993)

Leslie Nielsen's very funny spoof of golf instructional videos.

Bobby Jones: Stroke of Genius (2004)

A somewhat overly reverential but highly entertaining

portrait of one of the greatest champions. Anyone who values the traditions of the game will enjoy this beautifully mounted film.

The Greatest Game Ever Played (2005)

The inspiring true story of Francis Ouimet, the upstart amateur who bested Harry Vardon to win the U.S. Open. Nicely photographed with a good cast and the Disney touch.

Banning (1967)

Robert Wagner is a golf pro who is kicked off the tour for alleged cheating and is forced to hustle the country-club set to make a living, always keeping just one step ahead of a loan shark.

MOST WINS IN
PROFESSIONAL MAJORS

Through 2010

1. Jack Nicklaus
   (18: 6 Masters, 4 U.S. Opens, 3 British Opens, 5 PGAs)

2. Tiger Woods
   (14: 4 Masters, 3 U.S. Opens, 3 British Opens, 4 PGAs)

3. Walter Hagen
   (11: 2 U.S. Opens, 4 British Opens, 5 PGAs)

4. Ben Hogan
   (9: 2 Masters, 4 U.S. Opens, 1 British Open, 2 PGAs)

5. Gary Player
   (9: 3 Masters, 1 U.S. Open, 3 British Opens, 2 PGAs)

6. Tom Watson
   (8: 2 Masters, 1 U.S. Open, 5 British Opens)

7. Harry Vardon
   (7: 1 U.S. Open, 6 British Opens)

8. Gene Sarazen
   (7: 1 Masters, 2 U.S. Opens, 1 British Open, 3 PGAs)

9. Bobby Jones
   (7: 4 U.S. Opens, 3 British Opens)

10. Sam Snead
    (7: 3 Masters, 1 British Open, 3 PGAs)

11. Arnold Palmer
    (7: 4 Masters, 1 U.S. Open, 2 British Opens)

12. Nick Faldo
    (6: 3 Masters, 3 British Opens)

13. Lee Trevino
    (6: 2 U.S. Opens, 2 British Opens, 2 PGAs)

25 INDISPUTABLY GREAT
U.S. GOLF COURSES

- Pine Valley Golf Club, Pine Valley, New Jersey, designed by *George Crump* and *H.S. Cob*

- Augusta National Golf Club, Augusta, Georgia, designed by *Alister MacKenzie* and *Bobby Jones*

- Pebble Beach Golf Links, Pebble Beach, California, designed by *Jack Neville* and *Douglas Grant*

- Pinehurst Resort and Country Club, Pinehurst, North Carolina, designed by *Donald Ross*

- Shinnecock Hills Golf Club, Southampton, New York, designed by *William Flynn*

- The East Course at Merion Golf Club, Ardmore, Pennsylvania, designed by *Hugh Wilson*

- Medinah Country Club, Medinah, Illinois, designed by *Tom Bendelow*

- Muirfield Village Golf Club, Dublin, Ohio, designed by *Jack Nicklaus*

- Cypress Point Club, Pebble Beach, California, designed by *Alister MacKenzie* and *Robert Hunter*

- The West Course at Winged Foot Golf Club, Mamaroneck, New York, designed by *A. W. Tillinghast*

- Oakmont Country Club, Oakmont, Pennsylvania, designed by *Henry Fownes*

- National Golf Links of America, Southampton, New York, designed by *C.B. MacDonald*

- Seminole Golf Course, Juno Beach, Florida, designed by *Donald Ross*

- Oakland Hills Country Club, Bloomfield Hills, Michigan, designed by *Donald Ross* and *Robert Trent Jones*

- The Black Course at Bethpage State Park, Farmingdale, New York, designed by *Joseph H. Burbeck* and *A. W. Tillinghast*

- The Lower Course at Baltusrol Golf Club, Springfield, New Jersey, designed by *A. W. Tillinghast*

- The Ocean Course at Kiawah Island Golf Resort, Kiawah Island, South Carolina, designed by *Pete Dye*

- Bandon Dunes Golf Resort, Bandon, Oregon, designed by *David McLay Kidd*

- The Lake Course at the Olympic Club, San Francisco, California, designed by *Sam Whiting*

- Southern Hills Country Club, Tulsa, Oklahoma, designed by *Perry Maxwell*

- Riviera Country Club, Pacific Palisades, California, designed by *George C. Thomas* and *W.P. Bell*

- Spyglass Hill Golf Course, Pebble Beach, California, designed by *Robert Trent Jones*

- Colonial Country Club, Fort Worth, Texas, designed by *John Bredemus*

- The Stadium Course at Tournament Players Club at Sawgrass, Ponte Vedra Beach, Florida, designed by *Pete Dye*

- Harbor Town Golf Links, Hilton Head Island, South Carolina, designed by *Pete Dye* and *Jack Nicklaus*

20 INDISPUTABLY GREAT COURSES FROM THE REST OF THE WORLD

- The Old Course at St. Andrews Links, *St. Andrews, Scotland*

- Muirfield Golf Club, *Gullane, Scotland*

- The Royal Melbourne Golf Club, *Melbourne, Australia*

- The Old Course at Ballybunion Golf Club, *Ballybunion, Ireland*

- The Royal County Down Golf Club, *Newcastle, Northern Ireland*

- The Ailsa Championship Course at the Westin Turnberry Resort, *Turnberry, Scotland*

- The Royal St. George's Golf Club, *Sandwich, England*

- The Old Course at the Royal Troon Golf Club, *Troon, Scotland*

- Hirono Golf Club, *Kobe, Japan*

- Valderrama Golf Club, *San Roque, Spain*

- The Championship Course at Carnoustie Golf Links, *Carnoustie, Scotland*

- The Dunluce Course at the Royal Portrush Golf Club, *Portrush, Northern Ireland*

- The Royal Birkdale Golf Club, *Southport, England*

- Kingston Heath Golf Club, *Melbourne, Australia*

- The Old Course at Portmarnock Golf Club, *Portmarnock, Ireland*

- The Championship Course at Royal Dornoch Golf Club, *Dornoch, Scotland*

- Digby Pines Golf Resort and Spa, *Nova Scotia, Canada*

- The Old Course at Sunningdale Golf Club, *Sunningdale, England*

- Wack Wack Golf and Country Club, *Mandaluyong, the Philippines*

- Morfontaine Golf Club, *Senlis, France*

25 GREAT U.S. COURSES
THAT EVERYONE CAN PLAY

- Pebble Beach Golf Links, *Pebble Beach, California*

- Pinehurst Resort, *Pinehurst, North Carolina*

- Shadow Creek Golf Course, *Las Vegas, Nevada*

- Pacific Dunes, *Bandon, Oregon*

- Whistling Straits Golf Course, *Sheboygan, Wisconsin*

- Bandon Dunes Golf Resort, *Bandon, Oregon*

- The Black Course at Bethpage State Park, *Farmingdale, New York*

- The Ocean Course at Kiawah Island Golf Resort, *Kiawah Island, South Carolina*

- Spyglass Hill Golf Course, *Pebble Beach, California*

- Arcadia Bluffs Golf Course, *Arcadia, Michigan*

- Cog Hill Golf and Country Club, *Lemont, Illinois*

- Blackwolf Run Golf Course, *Kohler, Wisconsin*

- The Prince Course at the Princeville Golf Club, *Princeville, Kauai, Hawaii*

- Bay Hill Club and Lodge, *Orlando, Florida*

- The Cascades Course at the Homestead, *Hot Springs, Virginia*

- Harbor Town Golf Links, *Hilton Head Island, South Carolina*

- The Stadium Course at Tournament Players Club at Sawgrass, *Ponte Vedra Beach, Florida*

- Crosswater, *Sunriver, Oregon*

- Troon North, *Scottsdale, Arizona*

- Karsten Creek Course, *Stillwater, Oklahoma*

- PGA West Stadium Golf Course, *La Quinta, California*

- Torrey Pines Golf Course, *La Jolla, California*

- The Plantation Course at Kapalua Golf Resort, *Maui, Hawaii*

- The Broadmoor Golf Links, *Colorado Springs, Colorado*

- The Dunes Golf and Beach Club, *Myrtle Beach, South Carolina*

CLASSIC GOLF QUOTES

"It's nae gowff." *Allen Robertson* of St. Andrews, the first professional golfer of note, of the new "gutty" ball that replaced the feathery ball

"A man who can putt is a match for anyone." *Willie Park Sr.*

"If profanity had an influence on the flight of a ball, the game would be played far better than it is." *Horace Hutchinson*

"It's good sportsmanship not to pick up golf balls while they're still rolling." *Mark Twain*

"Did I make it look hard enough, son?" *Walter Hagen* to his caddy after a great recovery shot

"The more you play it, the less you know about it." *Patty Berg*

"Never hurry, never worry, and be sure to smell the flowers along the way." *Walter Hagen* on his philosophy about golf and life

"Bob Jones was a fine man to be partnered with in a tournament. He made you feel you were playing with a friend…and you were." *Gene Sarazen*

"As a young man he was able to stand up to just about the best life can offer, which is not easy, and later in life he stood up, with equal grace, to just about the worst." *Herbert Warren Wind* about the life of Bobby Jones

"Mr. Gene, you got to hit the 3-wood if you want to clear the water." *Stovepipe, Gene Sarazen's caddy* in the 1935 Masters. Sarazen hit a 4-wood, scoring his famous double eagle.

"In golf, when we hit a foul ball, we got to go out and play it." *Sam Snead* to fishing partner, Boston slugger Ted Williams

"Watson scares me. If he's lying six in the middle of the fairway, there's still some kind of way he will find to make a five." *Lee Trevino* on Tom Watson's ability to score

"Every day I try to tell myself that this is going to be fun today. I try to put myself in a great state of mind. Then I go out and screw it up with the first shot." *Johnny Miller* on his mental game plan

"The only equivalent plunge from genius I can think of was Ernest Hemingway's tragic loss of his ability to write. Hemingway got up one morning and shot himself. Nicklaus got up the next morning and shot a 66." *Ian Wooldridge* on Jack Nicklaus' 81–66 start in the British Open

5 THINGS GOLFERS YELL
INSTEAD OF "FORE!"

@*%&##!

*&#$#@!

%$$$**&!

&&´##@@!

Whoops!

GREAT GOLFERS, GREAT YEARS

1922: *Gene Sarazen* wins the U.S. Open and the PGA Championship among his 3 tour victories.

1924: *Walter Hagen* wins the British Open and the PGA Championship among his 5 tour victories.

1926: *Bobby Jones* wins the U.S. Open and the British Open.

1930: *Bobby Jones* wins the U.S. Open and the British Open, as well as the U.S. and British Amateur Championships; *Gene Sarazen* wins 8 tour events.

1932: *Gene Sarazen* wins the U.S. Open and the British Open among his 4 tour victories.

1933: *Paul Runyan* wins 9 tour events.

1934: *Paul Runyan* wins 7 tour events, including the PGA Championship.

1937: *Harry Cooper* wins 8 tour events.

1938: *Sam Snead* wins 8 tour events.

1939: *Henry Picard* wins 8 tour events, including the PGA Championship.

1941: *Craig Wood* wins the Masters and the U.S. Open; *Sam Snead* wins 7 tour events.

1944: *Byron Nelson* wins 8 tour events.

1945: *Byron Nelson* wins 18 tour events (11 in a row!) including the PGA Championship.

1946: *Ben Hogan* wins 13 tour events, including the PGA Championship.

1947: *Ben Hogan* wins 7 tour events.

1948: *Ben Hogan* wins the U.S. Open and the PGA Championship among his 10 tour victories.

1949: *Sam Snead* wins the Masters and the PGA Championship among his 6 tour victories; *Cary Middlecoff* wins 7 tour events, including the U.S. Open.

1950: *Sam Snead* wins 11 tour events.

1951: *Ben Hogan* wins the Masters and the U.S. Open among his 3 tour victories.

1953: *Ben Hogan* wins the Masters, the U.S. Open, and the British Open among his 5 tour victories.

1956: *Jack Burke* wins the Masters and the PGA Championship.

1960: *Arnold Palmer* wins the Masters and the U.S. Open among his 8 tour victories.

1962: *Arnold Palmer* wins the Masters and the British Open among his 8 tour victories.

1963: *Jack Nicklaus* wins the Masters and the PGA Championship among his 5 tour victories; *Arnold Palmer* wins 7 tour events.

1966: *Jack Nicklaus* wins the Masters and the British Open among his 3 tour victories.

1971: *Lee Trevino* wins the U.S. Open and the British Open among his 6 tour victories.

1972: *Jack Nicklaus* wins the Masters and the U.S. Open among his 7 tour victories.

1973: *Jack Nicklaus* wins 7 tour events, including the PGA Championship.

1974: *Johnny Miller* wins 8 tour events.

1975: *Jack Nicklaus* wins the Masters and the PGA Championship among his 5 tour victories.

1977: *Tom Watson* wins the Masters and the British Open among his 5 tour victories.

1980: *Tom Watson* wins 7 tour events, including the British Open; *Jack Nicklaus* wins the U.S. Open and the PGA Championship.

1982: *Tom Watson* wins the U.S. Open and the British Open among his 4 tour victories.

1990: *Nick Faldo* wins the Masters and the British Open.

1994: *Nick Price* wins the British Open and the PGA Championship among his 6 tour victories.

1998: *Mark O'Meara* wins the Masters and the British Open.

1999: *Tiger Woods* wins 8 tour events, including the PGA Championship.

2000: *Tiger Woods* wins the U.S. Open, the British Open, and the PGA Championship among his 9 tour victories.

2002: *Tiger Woods* wins the Masters and the U.S. Open, among his 5 tour victories.

2004: *Vijay Singh* wins 9 tour events, including the PGA Championship.

2005: *Tiger Woods* wins the Masters and the British Open, among his 6 tour victories.

2006: *Tiger Woods* wins the British Open and the PGA Championship among his 8 tour victories.

2007: *Tiger Woods* wins the PGA Championship among his 7 tour victories.

2008: *Padraig Harrington* wins the British Open and the PGA Championship.

10 BEST EXCUSES FOR WHY
YOU PLAYED SO POORLY

- That 71 I shot yesterday at Pebble Beach must have really taken it out of me.

- My clubs are being regripped. I borrowed this set.

- I tend to play down to the level of my competition.

- The course marshal looked at me funny.

- Are these holes regulation size? They seem small to me.

- I need a new set of clubs. Clearly these don't work.

- This course is in horrible condition.

- My chiropractor told me not to make a full turn so I wouldn't hurt my back.

- I kept hitting it into the woods so I could get more practice at trouble shots.

- I've been getting golf tips from a book called *A Pocket Guide for Golfers.*

16 GREAT DESTINATIONS
FOR A GOLF VACATION

(Places with great courses you can play
and good accommodations)

1. Monterey, California *(Pebble Beach, Spyglass Hill, the Links at Spanish Bay)*

2. St. Andrews, Scotland *(the Old Course, the New Course, Jubilee, and Kingsbarns)*

3. Pinehurst, North Carolina *(Pinehurst has 8 courses; number 2 is the highlight)*

4. Northern Ireland *(Royal Portrush, Royal County Down, Castlerock)*

5. Phoenix, Arizona *(Troon North, the Boulders, Grayhawk)*

6. Myrtle Beach, South Carolina *(the Dunes, Caledonia, Heritage)*

7. Hilton Head, South Carolina *(Harbour Town, Palmetto Dunes)*

8. Palm Springs and Palm Desert, California *(PGA West, La Quinta, Mission Hills)*

9. Maui and Lanai, Hawaii *(Kapalua, Wailea, Royal New Kent)*

10. Whistler, British Columbia, Canada *(Big Sky, Chateau Whistler, Nicklaus North)*

11. Orlando, Florida *(Bay Hill, Grand Cypress, Disney)*

12. Bend, Oregon *(Crosswater, Black Butte, Eagle Crest)*

13. Northwest England *(Royal Birkdale, Royal Lytham and St. Annes, Hoylake)*

14. Sheboygan, Wisconsin *(Blackwolf Run, Whistling Straits)*

15. Southwest Scotland *(Turnberry, Prestwick, Royal Troon)*

16. The Oregon coast *(Bandon Dunes, Pacific Dunes, Sandpines)*

16 HUMOROUS OBSERVATIONS ABOUT THE GREATEST GAME

"If you call on God to improve the results of a shot while it is in motion, you are using 'an outside agency' and are subject to appropriate penalties under the rules of golf."

Henry Longhurst

"The only time my prayers are never answered is on the golf course."

Billy Graham

"The harder you work, the luckier you get."

Gary Player

"Golf is so popular simply because it is the best game in the world at which to be bad. At golf it is the bad player who gets the most strokes."

A.A. Milne

"The hardest shot is a mashie at ninety yards from the green, where the ball has to be played against an oak tree, bounces back into a sand trap, hits a stone, bounces on the green, and then rolls into the cup. That shot is so difficult I have only made it once."

Zeppo Marx

"Golf is an ineffectual attempt to direct an uncontrollable sphere into an inaccessible hole with instruments ill-adapted for the purpose."

Winston Churchill

"One of the advantages bowling has over golf is that you seldom lose a bowling ball."

Don Carter,
professional bowler

"Golf lacks something for me. It would be better if once in a while someone came up from behind and tackled you just as you were hitting the ball."

Harold "Red" Grange

"They say golf is like life, but don't believe them. Golf is more complicated than that."

Gardner Dickinson

"I have a tip that can take five strokes off anyone's game. It's called an eraser."

Arnold Palmer

"The least thing upsets him on the links. He missed short putts because of the uproar of butterflies in the adjoining meadows."

P.G. Wodehouse

"I used to play golf with a guy who cheated so badly that he once had a hole in one and wrote down zero on his scorecard."

Bob Bruce

"For most amateurs, the best wood in the bag is the pencil."

Chi Chi Rodriguez

"Golf is a game in which you yell fore, shoot six, and write down five."

Paul Harvey

"They call it golf because all the other four-letter words were taken."

Ray Floyd

"My career started slowly and then tapered off."

Gary McCord

UNUSUAL RULES FROM
AROUND THE WORLD

Nyanza Golf Club in British East Africa, circa 1950:
"If a ball comes to rest in dangerous proximity to
a hippopotamus or crocodile, another ball may be
dropped at a safe distance, no nearer the hole, without penalty."

A Rhodesian golf course, circa 1972: "A stroke may be
played again if interrupted by gunfire or sudden
explosion."

Jinga Golf Club in Uganda: "On the green, a ball lying
in a hippo footmark may be lifted and placed not
nearer the hole without penalty."

Bjorkliden Arctic Golf Club in Sweden: "If a reindeer eats
your ball, drop another where the incident occurred."

Castle Grove Country Club in Iowa: "If ball lands on a
cow pie, you must play it as it lies."

What Fore? a private course in Texas: "Don't use your
hands to retrieve your ball from the badger den on
the fifth hole."

Smedberg Pines Golf Course in California: "Bear drop-
pings count as a loose impediment."

Ernie Holzemer's Pasture Golf Course in North Dakota:
"Use your 7-iron to kill rattlesnakes."

Muskeg Meadows Golf Course in Alaska: "If a raven steals your ball, you may replace it with no penalty if you have a witness to the theft."

GREAT QUOTES ABOUT GOLF

"Golf courses are the answer to the world's problems. When I get out on that green carpet called a fairway and manage to poke the ball right down the middle, my surroundings look like a touch of heaven on earth."

Jimmy Demaret

"What other people may find in poetry or art museums, I find in the flight of a good drive."

Arnold Palmer

"What a beautiful place a golf course is. From the meanest country pasture to the Pebble Beaches and St. Andrews of the world, a golf course is to me a holy ground. I feel God in the trees and grass and flowers, in the rabbits and the birds and the squirrels, in the sky and the water. I feel I am at home."

Harvey Penick

"Golf tells you about character. Play a round of golf with someone, and you know them more intimately than you might from years of dinner parties."

Harvey Penick

"Golf is the infallible test...The man who can go into a patch of rough alone, with the knowledge that only

God is watching him, and play his ball where it lies is the man who will serve you faithfully and well."

P.G. Wodehouse

"Golf is 20 percent mechanics and technique. The other 80 percent is philosophy, humor, tragedy, romance, melodrama, companionship, camaraderie, cussedness, and conversation."

Grantland Rice

"On the golf course, a man may be the dogged victim of inexorable fate, be struck down by an appalling stroke of tragedy, become the hero of an unbelievable melodrama, or the clown in a sidesplitting comedy—any of these within a few hours, and all without having to bury a corpse or repair a tangled personality."

Bobby Jones

12 TRAITS OF "REAL" GOLFERS

- Real golfers don't say tee box, they say tee.

- Real golfers don't say, "I'm going golfing today." They say, "I'm gonna play today."

- Real golfers do not have ball retrievers in their bags.

- Real golfers would still wear metal cleats if country club committees hadn't ruled them out.

- Real golfers wouldn't use pencils with erasers if country club committees hadn't bought them.

- Real golfers do not use funky gizmos to mark their balls. They use dimes, which, by the way, only cost a dime.

- Real golfers still replace divots and maybe even pour sand into them.

- Real golfers don't talk (or whisper) while others are hitting.

- Real golfers fix two ball marks on every green— theirs and one more.

- Real golfers carry a rule book and some rain gear in their bags.

- Real golfers rake a bunker so it is better after they played a shot than before.

- Real golfers have soil-free grooves in their irons.

WINNERS OF THE MOST LPGA MAJOR CHAMPIONSHIPS

Through 2010

Patty Berg (15)

Mickey Wright (13)

Louise Suggs (11)

Annika Sorenstam (10)

Babe Zaharias (10)

Betsy Rawls (8)

Karrie Webb (7)

Juli Inkster (7)

Kathy Whitworth (6)

Patty Sheehan (6)

Betsy King (6)

Pat Bradley (6)

10 THINGS TO CONSIDER
WHEN PLANNING A SHOT

- The wind direction and speed, the club's loft, and the height of your shot.

- The moisture and length of grass under the ball.

- The type of lie: uphill, downhill, side hill, or a combination of those.

- The receptiveness of the landing area.

- The best position to leave the ball for the next shot.

- The club selection that will best help to avoid bunkers, water, and other hazards.

- The risk of attempting a more difficult and rewarding shot instead of a safer but less rewarding one.

- The desired flight of the ball: draw or fade, high or low.

- The best club to hit and the force of your swing.

- The quality of your swing control on that round.

OVERHEARD BETWEEN GOLFERS AND THEIR CADDIES

Golfer: "I've played so poorly all day...I'm going to go drown myself in that lake."

Caddy: "I don't think you could keep your head down that long."

Golfer: "I'd move heaven and earth to be able to break 100."

Caddy: "Try heaven. You've already moved plenty of earth."

Golfer: "How do you like my game?"

Caddy: "I prefer golf."

Golfer: "I've never played this badly before!"

Caddy: "You've played before?"

Golfer: "Do you think my game is improving?"

Caddy: "Sure. You miss the ball much closer than you used to."

Golfer: "Please stop checking your watch all the time. It's distracting!"

Caddy: "This isn't a watch. It's a compass."

Golfer: "That can't be my ball. It looks far too old."
Caddy: "It's a long time since we started."

Golfer: "Do you think I can get there with a 5-iron?"
Caddy: "Eventually."

Golfer: "You've got to be the worst caddy in the world!"
Caddy: "I doubt it. That would be too much of a coincidence."

10 TIPS FOR BETTER CHIPPING

1. The more you hit down on the ball, the higher it goes.

2. Grip the club harder on chip shots than on a full swing.

3. Don't let your left wrist break on the forward swing of a chip. (Left-handers: Don't let your right wrist break on the forward swing of a chip.)

4. Play the ball off your back foot so you hit the ball crisply.

5. Listen for the ball to hit the green—don't watch for it to.

6. Hit the ball with an authoritative "pop." Don't hit it with a slow clubhead.

7. Keep the clubface hooded on the backswing—don't open it up.

8. Take numerous practice swings beside the ball to gauge the resistance of the grass.

9. Think about where your target is as you chip—don't think of mechanics.

10. Practice the same chip 100 times. Then find another one and practice it 100 times. And do it again. You'll probably have to hit one of them every time you play.

> "I have proved to myself what I have always said—that a good golfer doesn't have to be born that way. He can be made.
> I was, and practice is what made me—practice and tough, unrelenting labor."
>
> **BEN HOGAN**

16 TIPS ON COURSE MANAGEMENT

- When at a new course, find the pro or an experienced local caddie and ask him or her to fill you in on local knowledge.

- Think two shots ahead.

- Consider what the golf course architect was intending when he designed the hole you are about to play. Figure out where the architect is trying to make you hit it and where you should hit it.

- Determine ahead of time which are the birdie holes and the holes on which you should be content with par. Don't take foolish chances.

- Erase fairway bunkers by choosing the right club.

- Use enough club. Try hitting irons into the back fringe for a change. Most amateurs use just enough club so a perfect shot will barely make pin high, which means that anything less than a perfect shot is going to be farther from the hole.

- Play percentage golf. Take advantage of wide portions of the fairway and the fat part of the green.

- Find a level spot on the tee. Most tees have settled and are not flat all over.

- Tee up on the side of trouble and hit away from it.

- Know whether you are tending to fade or draw the ball on a given day and plan accordingly.

- Don't watch other players' swings.

- When riding in a cart, get out and walk whenever possible. Let the other guy drive.

- Talk to yourself. Try thinking, Birdie time! as you're teeing off. Your mind believes what you tell it.

- Don't get greedy. Respect the game; it can jump up and bite you—badly!

- Try to leave yourself gimme second putts if you miss the first. Tapping in and beginning to think about the next hole is much more enjoyable than stressing over a four-footer.

- Link your shots on a hole: Hit the fairway, hit the green. This simple philosophy is a time-tested strategy for winning.

WISECRACKS WE'VE OVERHEARD
ABOUT BAD GOLF SHOTS

- Get in! *(When a shot is not even remotely close.)*

- Fore in the Kmart! *(Wild drive.)*

- It's off the world! *(Really wild drive.)*

- That's good! Pick it up! *(When the group ahead is dreadfully slow and you're upset.)*

- Don't forget to write. *(When a putt goes way beyond the hole.)*

- Bring your toolbox. *(When a first putt requires a tough second putt.)*

- I don't think I've ever seen *that* before. *(On a really bizarre shot.)*

- You should take a couple weeks off and then quit.

HANDY GOLF EXCUSES

- My mother-in-law just lost her lease and moved in.

- I'm trying a new technique I just overheard on the lesson tee.

- My salmon salad didn't agree with me.

- Actually, I've only shot my average game once.

- My last set of clubs was lousy, and these aren't broken in yet.

- I can only play well when I have a caddy.

- I can't concentrate when other players rush me.

- These pin placements don't fit my shot shape. *(Evidently, the pins aren't in the woods.)*

- I'm trying out a new type of ball, and it's throwing my yardages off.

- I lack talent *(the only excuse never, ever spoken).*

15 WINNINGEST LPGA GOLFERS

As of January 1, 2011

Kathy Whitworth (88)

Mickey Wright (82)

Annika Sorenstam (72)

Patty Berg (60)

Louise Suggs (58)

Betsy Rawls (55)

Nancy Lopez (48)

JoAnne Carner (43)

Sandra Haynie (42)

Babe Zaharias (41)

Carol Mann (38)

Karrie Webb (36)

Patty Sheehan (35)

Betsy King (34)

Beth Daniel (33)

10 WAYS TO PSYCHE
OUT YOUR OPPONENT

1. Never lose your temper. To do so infuses your opponent with confidence.

2. When you miss a shot, look to the sky and laugh.

3. Whistle.

4. Learn to hit a 5-iron a 7-iron distance. Let your opponent see the club you hit.

5. When you're away, stand with your hands on your hips for 30 seconds or so, just staring at the target.

6. Concede short putts early in the round, and at a critical point in the match, turn away and make your opponent putt.

7. When your opponent is hitting, stand with your legs apart and your arms folded. Stare intently at him or her.

8. Don't initiate conversation. Keep talking to a minimum.

9. When in the lead, don't become sympathetic. Finish your opponent off.

10. If you are way behind in a match, try a risky shot in hopes of turning the tide.

10 CLASSIC GOLF JOKES

On returning home from a round of golf, a guy tells his wife, "Bad day at the course. Charlie had a heart attack on the third hole."

"That's terrible!" she says.

"You're telling me," he replies. "All day long it was hit the ball, drag Charlie, hit the ball, drag Charlie…"

A golfer hits a big slice on the first hole, and his ball ends up behind a small shed. He's about to chip out when the caddie says, "Wait, I'll open the window and the door, and you can hit a 5-wood right through the shed."

The caddie opens them up and the golfer takes a mighty swing. The ball nearly makes it through, but it hits the windowsill, ricochets off, and hits the golfer in the head.

The next thing he knows, he is standing at the pearly gates. St. Peter sees him with the 5-wood still in his hand and quips, "I guess you think you're a pretty good golfer, huh?"

"Well," the golfer says, "I got here in two, didn't I?"

A retiree received a set of golf clubs from his former coworkers. He asked the local pro for lessons, explaining that he knew nothing whatever of the game.

The pro showed him the stance and swing, and then he said, "Just hit the ball toward the flag on the first green."

The novice teed up and smacked the ball straight down the fairway and onto the green, where it stopped inches from the hole.

"Now what?" the fellow asked the speechless pro.

After he was able to speak again, the pro finally said, "Uh...you're supposed to hit the ball into the cup."

The beginner was disgusted. "Oh great! *Now* you tell me."

A couple of buddies decide to play together for the first time.

Mac is an avid golfer, and Jimmy is new to the game.

On the way to the course, Mac asks, "By the way, what's your handicap?"

Jimmy replies, "I don't have one...it's more like a permanent disability."

A guy walks up to some excruciatingly slow golfers and hands them a card that says, "I'm a deaf-mute. Can I play through?"

"Bug off," they tell him rudely. "You can wait like anyone else."

On the next hole, a ball flies into the group and hits one of the slow golfers right in the head. As he lies on the ground rubbing his head, the others look back to see who hit the shot. The deaf guy has a driver in one hand and is holding up four fingers with the other.

On Yom Kippur a rabbi sneaks out to play a solo round of golf. On the fifth hole he scores an ace. Looking down from heaven, an angel turns to God and asks, "How could you reward him that way for playing golf on such a holy day?"

God smiles and says, "Who's he gonna tell?"

A golfer hits a huge slice off the first tee. The ball sails over a fence and onto a highway where it hits a car, causing it to crash into a tree.

The stunned golfer rushes into the golf shop and shouts, "Help! Help! I just hit a terrible slice off the first tee, and it hit a car and caused a wreck! What should I do?"

The pro pauses a moment and then replies, "Try a slightly stronger grip."

A guy called his friend and asked him if he wanted to go out and play a round. His friend responded, "I am the master of my home—I can play golf whenever I want to. But hold on just a moment, and I'll find out if I want to."

A woman's husband asks her, "If I were to die, would you get married again and share our bed with your new husband?"

"I guess I might," she says.

"What about my car?" he asks. "Would you give that to him?"

"Perhaps," she answers.

"Would you give my golf clubs to him too?" he asks.

"No, of course not," she replies.

"Why not?" asks the husband.

"He's left-handed."

A fellow comes home after his regular Saturday golf game, and his wife asks why he doesn't include Tom O'Brien in the games anymore.

The husband asks, "Would you want to play with a guy who regularly cheats, swears up a storm over everything, lies about his score, and has nothing good to say about anyone else on the course?"

"Of course I wouldn't," replies the wife.

"Well," says the husband, "neither would Tom O'Brien."

18 INDISPUTABLY
GREAT GOLF HOLES

- The third at the Lake Course at the Olympic Club, San Francisco, California, a 223-yard par 3

- The fourth at Riviera Country Club, Pacific Palisades, California, a 236-yard par 3

- The eighth at Pebble Beach Golf Links, Pebble Beach, California, a 431-yard par 4

- The ninth at Pebble Beach Golf Links, Pebble Beach, California, a 464-yard par 4

- The twelfth at Augusta National Golf Club, Augusta, Georgia, a 155-yard par 3

- The thirteenth at Augusta National Golf Club, Augusta, Georgia, a 485-yard par 5

- The thirteenth at Pine Valley Golf Club, Pine Valley, New Jersey, a 448-yard par 4

- The fourteenth at Muirfield Village Golf Club, Dublin, Ohio, a 363-yard par 4

- The fourteenth at Shinnecock Hills Golf Club, Southampton, New York, a 447-yard par 4

- The fifteenth at Pine Valley Golf Club, Pine Valley, New Jersey, a 591-yard par 5

- The fifteenth at Harbor Town Golf Links, Hilton Head Island, South Carolina, a 575-yard par 5

- The sixteenth at Shinnecock Hills Golf Club, Southampton, New York, a 542-yard par 5

- The sixteenth at Cypress Point Club, Pebble Beach, California, a 219-yard par 3

- The seventeenth at Cypress Point Club, Pebble Beach, California, a 393-yard par 4

- The seventeenth at the Stadium Course at Tournament Players Club at Sawgrass, Ponte Vedra Beach, Florida, a 132-yard par 3

- The eighteenth at the East Course at Merion Golf Club, Ardmore, Pennsylvania, a 463-yard par 4

- The eighteenth at the Blue Course at Doral Golf Resort, Miami, Florida, a 443-yard par 4

- The eighteenth at Pebble Beach Golf Links, Pebble Beach, California, a 548-yard par 5

10 SECRETS TO HELP YOUR GAME

1. Keep a towel on your bag with a soaking-wet end. During play in hot weather, wet your hand (or hands if you don't wear a glove) and let it dry. This creates a tacky sensation that will improve your grip and reduce slipping.

2. If you use rubber grips, scrub them often with water and steel wool and dry them thoroughly to make them slip proof.

3. Take the time to use a tee to clean out the grooves of your irons before playing a shot. Backspin is important, and clean grooves create more spin.

4. In the rain, keep a dry towel in the ribs of your umbrella. Keep two or three extras handy in your bag if rain is possible.

5. Practice your short game with the same ball you play with, not with range balls. Practicing with a different brand of ball is analogous to practicing with a different set of clubs.

6. Eat lightly before you play, and snack on healthy foods during the round. Never let yourself become dehydrated.

7. To score your best, keep your mind on the game from the first tee to the eighteenth green. This means no chitchat, no anger, and no picking up instead of finishing a hole. To succeed at this level of concentration, find playing partners who have the same goal in mind—to score well.

8. Before teeing off, walk slowly, talk slowly, take your head cover off slowly, and practice your swing slowly. This will help you to make slower swings throughout the round.

9. Define ten shots you need to play your best golf. Then, over the course of a month, spend an entire day—six or eight hours—on each of them. Few players other than professionals have ever dedicated eight hours to, for example, hitting out of a greenside bunker. A single day in the bunker may make you the best bunker player in your club.

10. Go to a tour event and absorb the tempo and techniques of the professional players. Believe it or not, a good swing can be contagious. Study the greats in person. Something might rub off on you!

10 IMPORTANT
GOLF ETIQUETTE RULES

———————

- Never stand directly behind a player who is teeing off.

- Be ready when it's your turn to play.

- Silence is golden when someone is playing a shot.

- Always rake a bunker, leaving it better than you found it.

- Never walk up the face of a bunker; exit the rear side.

- Never stand within eyesight of a player who is putting.

- When tending a pin, hold the flag and make sure the pin is loose in the cup.

- When you remove the pin, place it gently in the fringe area.

- When using a golf cart, always park to the rear of the green.

- Play without delay. Keep your place on the course.

10 WAYS TO GET MORE OUT OF YOUR PRACTICE SESSION

1. Work on one fundamental at a time.

2. Only hit one shot per minute, using a full, pre-swing routine.

3. Practice with the same ball you use during the round.

4. Employ full concentration on every shot. Focus on quality, not quantity.

5. Don't get sloppy. Take a break and start again.

6. Practice a particular type of shot until you know you can produce it at will.

7. Don't be afraid to try new things. Trial and error produces new knowledge.

8. Don't practice to the point of injury. Know your limits.

9. Make it fun.

10. Write notes in a journal after each session, trying to capture the feel.

THE PAST TEN MAJOR CHAMPIONSHIP WINNERS

The Masters

2001—Tiger Woods
2002—Tiger Woods
2003—Mike Weir
2004—Phil Mickelson
2005—Tiger Woods
2006—Phil Mickelson
2007—Zach Johnson
2008—Trevor Immelman
2009—Angel Cabrera
2010—Phil Mickelson

The U.S. Open

2001—Retief Goosen
2002—Tiger Woods
2003—Jim Furyk
2004—Retief Goosen
2005—Michael Campbell
2006—Geoff Ogilvy
2007—Angel Cabrera
2008—Tiger Woods
2009—Lucas Glover
2010—Graeme McDowell

The British Open

2001—David Duval
2002—Ernie Els
2003—Ben Curtis
2004—Todd Hamilton
2005—Tiger Woods
2006—Tiger Woods
2007—Padraig Harrington
2008—Padraig Harrington
2009—Stewart Cink
2010—Louis Oosthuizen

The PGA Championship

2001—David Toms
2002—Rich Beem
2003—Shaun Micheel
2004—Vijay Singh
2005—Phil Mickelson
2006—Tiger Woods
2007—Tiger Woods
2008—Padraig Harrington
2009—Y.E. Yang
2010—Martin Kaymer

5 GREAT MOMENTS OF THE U.S. AMATEUR CHAMPIONSHIP

1. *Francis Ouimet,* who beat Harry Vardon and Ted Ray in the 1913 Open, and who won the Amateur in 1914, wins it again in 1931 at Beverly Country Club.

2. *Lawson Little* wins both the British and U.S. Amateurs in 1934 and again in 1935.

3. *Charles B. MacDonald* wins the very first U.S. Amateur at Shinnecock in 1895.

4. *Bobby Jones* completes the Grand Slam at Merion in 1930.

5. *Jack Nicklaus* warns the golf world that he is coming by winning the Amateur in 1959 and 1961.

10 GREAT SWING TIPS

1. Play golf on shock absorbers, not stilts. Keep your knees flexed when you address the ball.

2. Swing shoulder to shoulder. Feel your left shoulder under your chin at the top of your backswing and your right shoulder under your chin at and past impact. (*Left-handers:* substitute left for right and right for left.)

3. Watch the club strike the ball. Then allow your head to rotate to the target.

4. Swing the driver with the intent of sweeping the ball up, leaving the tee intact.

5. The first move of your backswing should be your shirt placket turning away from your target; the first move of your downswing should be your belt buckle turning back toward the hole.

6. Trust your swing. Fear and indecision usually lead to an incomplete shoulder turn.

7. Finish your swing up on your right toe with your belt buckle toward the target. (*Left-handers:* substitute left for right.)

8. Kick your right knee toward the target on the downswing. (*Left-handers:* substitute left for right.)

9. The more you hit down on a ball, the higher it goes.

10. Don't start your downswing until you know you have finished your backswing.

LAST 10 WINNERS OF WOMEN'S
MAJOR CHAMPIONSHIPS

Kraft Nabisco Championship

2001—Annika Sorenstam
2002—Annika Sorenstam
2003—Patricia Meunier-Lebouc
2004—Grace Park
2005—Annika Sorenstam
2006—Karrie Webb
2007—Morgan Pressel
2008—Lorena Ochoa
2009—Brittany Lincicome
2010—Yani Tseng

LPGA Championship

2001—Karrie Webb
2002—Se Ri Pak
2003—Annika Sorenstam
2004—Annika Sorenstam
2005—Annika Sorenstam
2006—Se Ri Pak
2007—Suzann Pettersen
2008—Yani Tseng
2009—Anna Nordqvist
2010—Christine Kerr

U.S. Women's Open

2001—Karrie Webb
2002—Juli Inkster
2003—Hilary Lunke
2004—Meg Mallon
2005—Birdie Kim
2006—Annika Sorenstam
2007—Christie Kerr
2008—Inbee Park
2009—Eun Hee Ji
2010—Paula Creamer

Women's British Open

2001—Se Ri Pak
2002—Karrie Webb
2003—Annika Sorenstam
2004—Karen Stupples
2005—Jeong Jang
2006—Sherri Steinhauer
2007—Lorena Ochoa
2008—Ji-Yai Shin
2009—Catriona Matthew
2010—Yani Tseng

10 THINGS THAT WILL IMPROVE YOUR SAND PLAY

1. Don't swing an inch or two behind your ball; rather, move the ball an inch or two forward in your stance to hit behind the ball.

2. On buried lies, shut the clubface, hold on tight, and hit an inch or two behind the ball, leaving the wedge in the sand.

3. Imagine bunker shots as an attempt to shower the green with sand. The ball is just another grain of sand.

4. To hit a bunker shot 30 feet, swing as hard as you would to hit a fairway shot 30 yards.

5. On fairway bunker shots, minimize your hip turn on your backswing.

6. Make an abrupt wrist break on your backswing on sand shots.

7. With an open stance, take the club back on the outside on the backswing.

8. Dig your feet into the sand about an inch. This helps your footing on the shot, and it puts the club's arc an inch under your ball.

9. Spend an entire day in a bunker practicing, and you'll be likely to come out of it as an excellent bunker player.

10. Don't stare at the ball on explosion shots; stare a few inches behind the ball and hit that target.

"Golf puts a man's character on the anvil
and his richest qualities—patience,
poise, and restraint—to the flame."
BILLY CASPER

13 GREAT SHOTS IN GOLF HISTORY

1. *Young Tom Morris,* on his way to winning the 1868 British Open, makes the first hole in one in competition at the eighth hole at Prestwick, Scotland.

2. *Bobby Jones* calls a stroke on himself as his ball moves at address in the second round of the 1926 U.S. Open at Scioto in Columbus, Ohio. Jones disdained the approval he got for this act, saying, "To praise one for following the rules is like congratulating someone for not robbing a bank." Jones birdies the seventy-second hole to edge Joe Turnesa by a shot.

3. With a 40-foot putt, *Bobby Jones* wins the 1930 U.S. Open at Interlachen, Minnesota—a key stroke in his Grand Slam of the U.S. Open and Amateur and the British Open and Amateur.

4. *Gene Sarazen* hits a 4-wood on April 7, 1935, at the fifteenth at Augusta National Golf Club. The ball went into the hole for a double eagle, erasing Craig Wood's three-shot lead. Sarazen's "shot heard 'round the world" leads him to a win in a 36-hole playoff for the second Masters tournament.

5. *Ben Hogan* hits a 1-iron at the seventy-second hole of the 1950 U.S. Open at Merion Cricket Club. The shot finds the final green for a two-putt par and a slot in the playoff with Lloyd Mangrum and George Fazio, which Hogan wins. His legs ache the entire time because of a horrendous automobile accident that threatened his life and kept him on his back in the hospital for two months just a year before.

6. *Lew Worsham* hits a 135-yard wedge shot to the final hole at the Tam O'Shanter Club's World Championship in 1953. The shot goes in the hole in the first televised golf event, giving him a one-shot victory over Chandler Harper as millions watch at home.

7. *Arnold Palmer*, after a long birdie at the seventy-first hole in the 1960 Masters, hits a perfect 6-iron shot to a few feet from the pin and makes the putt, robbing Ken Venturi of a green coat with a charge that becomes his trademark.

8. *Arnold Palmer* asks writer Bob Drum, "What would a 65 do?" during the break between the 36-hole U.S. Open final rounds at Cherry Hills in 1960. Drum replies, "Nothing!" infuriating Palmer. Arnold then drives the par-4 first hole,

something he had tried and failed to do during the first three rounds, and he two putts for a birdie. He then birdies five of the next six holes for a front-round 30, a 65 for the day, and the Open. The "Arnold Palmer charge" is born that year.

9. On the seventy-first hole of the 1972 U.S. Open at Pebble Beach, *Jack Nicklaus* absolutely ices another open title by hitting a 1-iron to inches of the hole. He later remarks that on the top of his backswing he thought he might hit it into the Pacific Ocean on the left. He made a mid-swing correction that became one of his greatest shots.

10. On that same seventy-first hole at Pebble Beach in 1982, *Tom Watson's* 2-iron winds up in the deep rough near the left rear pin placement. Jack Nicklaus is in the clubhouse with a chance to set the golf world on its ear with a record fifth U.S. Open title. Watson needs two pars coming in for a tie and probably the greatest playoff in golf history. But the Stanford graduate who had admittedly snuck onto Pebble as a student declares to his caddy, "I'm not going to try and get this one close; I'm going to hole it." And he does. After a 3-wood, 7-iron, 9-iron safe

approach to 20 feet on the par five eighteenth, he hit his first putt hard, scaring him. But it hits the hole and goes in, and he wins by two shots. Nicklaus, deflated but still the sportsman, has some interesting words with Tom on the green, which only those two heard.

11. Greg Norman, fresh off his British Open win at Turnberry, stands on the eighteenth tee at the PGA Championship at Inverness in Toledo with second-year pro *Bob Tway*, the two all square. Norman's wedge to the par-4 eighteenth backs up into the tall rough fringe. Bob Tway's wedge finds the right greenside bunker. Tway then proceeds to hole his bunker shot, leaving Norman to watch the tournament go to Tway.

12. At Augusta in 1987, Greg Norman's rash of birdies on the final nine gains him a spot in a three-way playoff with local boy *Larry Mize* and Seve Ballesteros. Ballesteros three-putts the par-4 tenth and is eliminated. On hole 11, the second playoff hole, Larry Mize plays, as Ben Hogan always did, to a spot to the right of the green, avoiding the lake on the left. He then chips in on Norman, who could not make a long birdie putt to tie. In eight months Norman saw two off-green hole-outs take

major hopes from him. To his credit, Norman handled the loss with a smile despite a second cruel loss in less than a year. In his career, Norman lost a playoff in all four majors.

13. With putts of 25 and 6 feet on the seventieth and seventy-first holes of the 1999 U.S. Open at Pinehurst, *Payne Stewart* needs an 18-footer for par to beat Phil Mickelson, his playing partner. In his trademark knickers, Hogan-style cap, and a waterproof jacket with the sleeves cut off for better swing freedom, Stewart holes the putt for his second Open and final victory. (Later that year, a month after playing in his fifth Ryder Cup, Stewart's chartered private jet loses oxygen and crashes, killing all onboard.)

12 PEOPLE WHO GREATLY INFLUENCED THE GAME OF GOLF

- *Old Tom Morris* was the most respected man in Scottish golf.

- *John Reid*, the father of American golf, laid out the first U.S. golf course in St. Andrews, New York.

- *Francis Ouimet*, an amateur who lived across the street from the Country Club in Brookline, Massachusetts, found himself tied for the 1913 U.S. Open there with Ted Ray and Harry Vardon, two golf icons of the day. He beat them both handily in an 18-hole playoff.

- *Walter Hagen,* whose cheeky antics included arriving at a tournament in a Rolls Royce, was instrumental in lifting the status of golf professionals, who previously were not admitted into the clubhouse during a tournament.

- In 1928, Texan *Jack O'Brien* put up a $5000 purse for the inaugural Texas Open, which became the beginning of today's pro tour.

- *Gene Sarazen* revolutionized golf with a little solder on the bottom of a Wilson pitching wedge. After flying with friend Howard Hughes, Gene realized that the airplane wing was the ideal model for his new sand wedge, which had a flange that guided the clubhead in and out of the sand rather than cut into the sand, as did a pitching wedge.

- After a peerless amateur career, *Bobby Jones* built the Augusta National Golf Club and created the finest golf tournament in the world—the Masters.

- Through endless practice, *Ben Hogan* discovered exactly how to use the skeletal and muscular systems of the human body to create amazing shot results with a golf club and ball.

- *Mildred "Babe" Zaharias*, an Olympic gold medalist and silver medalist in javelin, hurdles, and high jump, was a founding member of the LPGA. She was named "Female Athlete of the Year" by the Associated Press in 1932, 1945, 1946, 1947, 1950, and 1954. She won 10 LPGA major championships and was considered the best female athlete of her time. The other founding members: Bettye Danoff, Marlene Bauer Hagge, Marilynn Smith, Shirley Spork, Louise Suggs, Alice Bauer, Patty Berg, Helen

Dettweiler, Helen Hicks, Opal Hill, Betty Jameson, and Sally Sessions.

- *Arnold Palmer's* exciting brand of golf stirred a nation and created a new level of interest in the game.

- *Jack Nicklaus* became the greatest player the game has ever seen.

- *Tiger Woods'* incredible brand of golf brought the youth of America into the game. He may surpass Jack Nicklaus as the greatest player the game has ever seen.

10 GREAT BOOKS ABOUT GOLF

- *Harvey Penick's Little Red Book* by Harvey Penick.
  Simple lessons from one of golf's greatest
  teachers.

- *Five Lessons: The Modern Fundamentals of Golf*
  by Ben Hogan
  Advanced lessons from one of the all-time
  greatest players.

- *A Good Walk Spoiled* by John Feinstein
  A behind-the-scenes look at the world of
  professional golf.

- *The Majors* by John Feinstein
  Another fascinating peek inside the ropes,
  this time focusing on the majors.

- *The Golf Omnibus* by P.G. Wodehouse
  The classic British humorist offers hilarious
  short stories about golf and those who are
  obsessed by it.

- *Golf in the Kingdom* by Michael Murphy
  A wonderfully atmospheric novel about the
  mystical side of this great game.

- *Dead Solid Perfect* by Dan Jenkins
  This ribald and witty novel about hustlers and pros is one of the funniest books about golf.

- *Golf Dreams* by John Updike
  One of America's finest novelists reflects on his love for the game.

- *Golf My Way* by Jack Nicklaus
  One of the very best explains every aspect of the game with amazing clarity.

- *Golf Is Not a Game of Perfect* by Bob Rotella
  A peerless examination of the mental side of the game by a sports psychologist who works with many successful pros.

CHARACTER QUALITIES DEVELOPED BY PLAYING GOLF

- *Patience:* Golf demands that we be patient with ourselves, other players, and the bad luck that sometimes strikes every golfer.

- *Courage:* Sometimes we have to have the courage to attempt things that are beyond us.

- *Humility:* Knowing your limits is important. Golf is quick to remind you.

- *Discipline:* Hard work, practice, and goal-setting are essential to improvement.

- *Creativity:* Sometimes you need to think outside the box to achieve your goals.

- *Focus:* The single-minded concentration needed for golf can come in handy for other areas of life.

- *Honesty:* Do you improve your lie when no one is looking or do you call a deserved penalty on yourself even when no one else sees?

- *Perseverance:* You have to keep playing—even through adversity, a temporary loss of skill, or when you hit a patch of bad luck.

- *A sense of humor:* If you can't laugh at yourself, golf is not a recommended activity.

CLASSIC QUOTES ABOUT GOLF

"Don't touch it, Lord. It'll
cost him two strokes."

LEE TREVINO,
after a pro-am partner skied his tee shot

"I want to live to 112 so I can shoot my age."

AUTHOR UNKNOWN

"My game's improving. My whiffs
are much closer to the ball."

JACK LEMMON

"The reason the pro tells you to keep your
head down is so you can't see him laughing."

PHYLLIS DILLER

"I would like to deny all allegations by Bob
Hope that during my last game of golf,
I hit an eagle, a birdie, an elk, and a moose."

GERALD FORD

"Don't be too proud to take lessons. I'm not."

JACK NICKLAUS

"The more I practice, the luckier I get."

BEN HOGAN

"Luck? Sure. But only after long practice and
only with the ability to think under pressure."

MILDRED "BABE" DIDRIKSON ZAHARIAS

"Correct one fault at a time. Concentrate
on the one fault you want to overcome."

SAM SNEAD

"Success in golf depends less on
strength of body than upon strength
of mind and character."

ARNOLD PALMER

RICK'S 101 AMAZINGLY SIMPLE TIPS

Note: Left-handed players need to reverse instructions related to specific body movements.

1 For any golfer, the first shot often foreshadows the entire day.

An exceptionally good first drive may inspire you to new heights, and an embarrassing one may undermine your confidence. Prepare for that crucial first swing. Before teeing off, stretch, hit practice balls, and visualize a perfect shot.

2 For every shot you hit on the practice range, hit three around the practice green.

Ninety percent of your ability to score depends on your performance from 30 yards in.

3 A half-hour before you tee off, do everything in slow motion.

Walk slowly; talk slowly; put your glove on slowly; breathe slowly; practice-swing very slowly; remove your head cover slowly. Then—your swing tempo for the day just might be slow.

4 To ensure correct positioning of the club at the top of your backswing, execute a swing and freeze at the top.

> Remove your left hand from the grip, holding it loosely with only your right hand. The club will drop. If the shaft lands between your neck and right shoulder, your swing plane is correct.

5 The club should be gripped in the fingers of your right hand.

> Make certain the lifeline of your right hand suffocates your left thumb, which should be straight down the top of the shaft.

6 Metaphorically, play golf on shock absorbers—*not* stilts.

> Make sure your legs are well-flexed, with your left knee pointing in toward the ball on the backswing. Kick your right knee toward the ball on the forward swing.

7 Swing shoulder-to-shoulder.

> Have your left shoulder under your chin at the top of your backswing. Feel your right

shoulder under your chin as the clubhead is three feet past impact.

8 **See the ball being struck by the clubhead.**

When striking a teed ball, keep your head in position long enough to see the tee after impact; then let your body-turn bring your head around to view the ball's flight.

9 **When aligning, aim your feet slightly to the left.**

Every player's tendency is to address the ball with their feet aiming to the right of the intended target line. This common error usually causes an incomplete shoulder turn as the player attempts to pull the shot back to the target.

10 **Promise yourself on the first tee that you will give every shot your full attention.**

If you miss a shot, dismiss it as your best effort—no regrets. Approach the next shot mentally in the present. If your thoughts are focused 100 percent on the shot at hand, you will have no room in your mind to think about previous errors.

11 Swing your driver with the intent of sweeping the ball up, leaving the tee intact.

> The driver is the only club in the bag that requires an additional piece of equipment (the tee). Because of the driver's low loft, one must make an extra effort to hit up on the ball.

12 The first move of your backswing should be your shirt placket turning away from your target; the first move of your downswing should be your belt buckle turning back toward the hole.

13 Fear and indecision about a shot usually lead to an incomplete shoulder turn.

> Trust your swing.

14 A bad shot often costs a player a few more strokes. A bad temper often costs a player his whole day.

> Whatever happens, try to remain calm.

15 If a particular hole intimidates you from the tee, pretend you are on the tee of a favorite similar hole and make that swing.

16 Golf course architects are paid big money to design golf puzzles.

Solve the puzzle on each hole before teeing off.

17 When preparing to play on an extremely windy day, add ten shots to par.

You'll play in a relaxed state of mind, and you'll shoot a lower score than many others.

18 To learn proper delayed hit (release), grip your driver upside down—with your hands near the clubhead—and swing normally.

Listen for a distinct swish sound created as you swing. Ensure that this noise occurs at or past where the ball would be on the ground.

19 Finish your swing completely up on your right toe with your belt buckle toward the target.

Hold your right foot perpendicular to the ground until the ball lands. This method cultivates perfect balance.

20 Here's the final word on excuses and bad luck: The ball goes where *you* hit it!

21 Address the ball against the sweet spot of the club.

If you don't think hitting the ball on the sweet spot is vital, bounce a ball on different spots of the clubface. When you hit the sweet spot, you may have to duck as the ball leaps off the clubface.

22 Your first putt on the practice green should be under one foot.

This technique starts your day off right. The sound of the ball rattling around in the cup is a powerful association of past success and puts you in a resourceful frame of mind. Lipping out your first few putts of the day can easily start a negative train of thought.

23 If you are having a spectacular round, stay loose and enjoy it—but realize that the bubble may burst at any time.

By keeping expectations at a reasonable level, you just might get to the clubhouse before the playing streak ends. In any round "golf giveth and golf taketh away," so keep smiling no matter what happens to the magic. When the round is over, go to the range and figure out what went right. Jot your findings down in a journal and use these insights later.

24 **Try to never hit two bad shots in a row.**

Make it a goal to always follow a bad shot with a good shot. It needn't be a career-best or heroic shot—just a good one.

25 **If you are going to play a shot safe, play it extremely safe.**

When you take a gamble, the reward should far outweigh the risk. A bogey is easier to take mentally and recover from than a triple bogey, which can demoralize you completely.

26 **Once a month, play nine holes with only a three iron, seven iron, sand wedge, and putter.**

You'll discover new facets of shot-making.

27 **A good exercise at the range is to hit your sand wedge as smoothly as you can.**

Try to hit all other clubs in your bag with the same smooth swing—starting with your pitching wedge. If you begin swinging too hard, do not advance to the next club until you regain the desired smoothness. Some days you can maintain the smoothness all the way through the driver, and some days you can't get past the eight iron. But whatever the outcome, you will have practiced good swing tempo.

28 **Golf is an expensive game.**

Visit your PGA professional and ask him to help you select the best equipment you can afford, thus maximizing your potential. A professional of today can muster a good score with ancient Hickory clubs only because he sports an excellent swing. The less talent you have, the more you need well-fitted equipment. For example, properly fitted shafts are essential to producing good golf shots. Weak shafts over-oscillate throughout the swing, causing shots to fly both left and right. You will not be able to fix this fault even with practice.

29   **Know whether your tee shots on a given day tend to draw or fade.**

If you are fading, aim down the left quarter of the fairway, using the other three-quarters as leeway; likewise, if you are drawing, aim for the right quarter of the fairway. Players who aim for the center of a fairway or directly at a flagstick have less room for error.

30   **Choose your club for pitching and chipping relative to how much running-room there is to the hole.**

The less running-room, the more loft is needed on the clubface. A highly lofted shot lands softer and stops quicker than a lowly lofted one; however, the less-lofted club lands with less backspin and is a more predictable shot. Select the club with the lowest loft that carries the ball safely onto the green and stops the ball near the hole.

31   **Hit down on *chips* and *pitches*.**

Trying to swing up on these shots—in an attempt to lift the ball up—is self-defeating. By hitting down on chips and pitches, you are assuring that the leading edge of the club-face will slide under the ball without skulling it (smacking the middle or top of the ball).

32 A sand wedge is not just for sand play.

To play a sand wedge from around the green, follow this formula:

- Choke the club to the end of the grip.

- Play the ball off your back foot.

- Grip the club very firmly and strike the ball with an authoritative "pop."

- Prevent your left wrist from hinging on the follow-through.

- Leave your head in position. *Listen* for the ball to hit the green before you look to see the results.

33 In a bunker, dig your feet about an inch into the sand.

There are two reasons for this: 1) your feet will be stable during your swing, enabling your club to consistently strike the same spot in the sand; and 2) the arc of your swing will travel through the sand about one inch under the ball, causing an effective explosion shot.

34 On sand shots, don't adjust your swing in order to hit behind the ball; instead, put the ball an inch or two forward in your stance.

35 When your ball is buried in a greenside bunker, shut the sand wedge's face 30 degrees.

Maintain a firm left-hand grip and strike one inch behind the ball with the hooded clubface. Because the clubface's toe is knifing into the sand—without the club's flange bouncing off the sand—the wedge continues downward and the ball is jettisoned up and out with no backspin. A little experimentation using this technique will arm you with a valuable new shot.

36 Imagine bunker shots as an attempt to shower the green with sand.

Pretend that your ball is just another grain among the sand. With that metaphor in mind, you'll be surprised how effortlessly your ball comes out.

37 **To hit a bunker shot 30 feet, swing as hard as you would to hit a fairway shot 30 yards.**

Many golfers under-swing on bunker shots because the brain resists swinging hard for a short shot. Overcome this tendency by forcing yourself to explode through the shot.

38 **When hitting out of fairway bunkers, minimize your hip-turn on the backswing.**

39 **When playing side hill lies, expect your ball's flight to follow the same direction that the ball would roll down the hill.**

A ball above your feet is likely to be pulled, and one below your feet is likely to be pushed.

40 **On uphill and downhill lies, let your left shoulder "follow the hill."**

In other words, on a downhill lie, your left shoulder should be low; on an uphill lie, your left shoulder should be high.

41 Never rush a short putt. Mark your ball and gather yourself before attempting any putt.

42 On short putts, *listen*—don't look—for the ball to go in.

43 Pick a line for a putt and believe in it.

Vividly visualize that line. You'll make a better stroke and more putts.

44 On putts, address the ball just inside your left foot.

Playing the ball too far back in your stance causes you to hit down on it. The ball will bounce all the way to the hole—and probably rim out of the cup.

45 *Always* accelerate through a putt.

46 A folding left wrist on the forward stroke of a short putt is a prescription for failure.

Keep the putter-head even with or behind your hands on short putts.

47 **Triangulate on breaking putts.**

On the side of the break, stand across from your ball. Step back until your ball, you, and the cup form the corners of an equilateral triangle. Once you reach this position, scrutinize the steepness of the hill. You will gain an overall perspective of the slope and distance of the putt.

48 **The putting expression "never up, never in" is misleading.**

A ball lingering at the edge of a cup is more likely to drop in than is one struck hard enough to run three feet by the hole. Leave yourself more tap-ins than three-footers.

49 **Buy a high-quality, correctly fitted putter and *marry* it!**

A player who frequently changes his putter is unable to cultivate a friendship with it. Bobby Jones had Calamity Jane; Ben Crenshaw uses Little Ben. Gary Player has carried the same beat-up black putter for years, and Jack Nicklaus logged most of his wins with his George Low model. A cumulative degree of effectiveness seems to be gained by sticking with the same putter for years on end.

50 Learn the unplayable lie rule and lateral water hazard rule well.

They will become your good friends. Interestingly, if you apply these rules properly, those who are unfamiliar with the rules of golf may accuse you of cheating!

51 Golf is a game for ladies and gentlemen.

You are your own judge and jury. Take as much pride in calling a tough ruling on yourself as you would in sinking a long putt. The golf course is one of the few places where a person's true character reveals itself for others to observe. Be impeccable!

52 People who cannot afford to play golf are probably faced with more challenges than those who can.

So let us all try to count our blessings—as well as our strokes—on the golf course. And remember—it's just a game!

53 **Most golf shots are missed before the club goes back!**

Learn to set up a "tripod" with exacting precision. Your feet and fully extended arms are the three legs of the tripod. First, set the clubface directly behind the ball and leave it there. Then place your feet into position, being certain that the pressure of your weight is slightly on your heels. Your weight should not be on your toes. Only then is it correct to move the clubhead to waggle (to settle into your stance). Using this exact address method, you will eliminate swing faults caused by imperfect balance.

54 **You will see *few* good golfers with a bad grip, and *fewer* bad golfers with a good grip.**

Let your arms hang in front of you while in an address posture. Bring your hands together and onto the club as if you were going to clap them. Then form your grip. This method will assure proper hand positioning relative to the clubface.

55 **Searching for a driver that gives you more distance is time well spent.**

> The golf expression, "Drive for show—putt for dough," is misleading. Increasing your tee shots by just 20 yards can make a vast difference in your scoring. Modern technology provides clubs that are superior to models of even a few years ago. It pays to keep updating your equipment—especially the driver.

56 **Your backswing should take approximately twice as long as your downswing.**

> A slow rhythmic backswing allows sufficient time for the body's muscle-memory to produce a consistent swing. Start your downswing only after you *know* you have finished your backswing!

57 **Tight arms decrease clubhead speed; loose, rope-like arms allow the clubhead to accelerate.**

> The waggle is a rehearsal for the backswing. Check for excess tension in your arms as you waggle. Squeeze tightly with your left pinky finger throughout the entire swing process.

58 **In every round there are surprises, both good and bad.**

Seasoned tour professionals have learned the importance of maintaining emotional equilibrium during championship play— but even they often struggle with it. *Always* expect the unexpected on the golf course.

59 **Practice to play, don't play to practice.**

Ben Hogan once stated that he was striking the ball as well as ever, but he had lost the knack of scoring. Practicing and scoring are two different matters. The objective is to be prepared for a day of battle on the course.

60 **On fairway iron shots, select a club that when struck perfectly lands the ball *beyond* the hole.**

In this way, a slightly less-than-perfect shot will land the ball closer to the flagstick. If you choose a club that must be struck perfectly *to reach* pin-high, a less-than-perfect shot will land the ball farther away from the hole.

61 When teeing off in a strong downwind, consider using a 4 wood.

The added spin will rocket the ball upward into the draft, allowing the wind to carry the ball farther.

62 If a par 4 with reachable fairway bunkers does not require length off the tee, you can take the bunkers out of play by hitting a club that lands the ball just short of them.

Evaluate every hole. Don't let the golf course designer trick you into making a tactical error.

63 Straight tee shots and skillfully executed first putts are vital factors to scoring well. Practice accordingly.

64 The goal of the tee shot on a par 4 is to make the remainder of the hole the easiest possible par 3.

The goal of the tee shot on a par 5 is to make the remainder of the hole the easiest possible par 4.

65 Every shot makes somebody happy.

In match play an obvious display of shaken confidence or displeasure over a poor shot boosts your opponent's morale. If, instead, you greet that lousy shot with a smile and a carefree laugh, you can shake your opponent's confidence.

66 Someone coined the phrase, "Trees are 90 percent air."

Well guess what—just left, right, or above a tree is 100 percent air. Time spent on the range learning to work the ball left, right, high, and low will come in quite handy on the course.

67 When it's breezy, hit 'em easy.

68 Most golfers do not know the distance each of their clubs carries a ball on the fly.

Designate five practice balls for each club by writing the club's number on them. Hit the balls on a range with wet turf. Check the yardages to see how far, on average, each club will fly the ball into the air. This is *necessary* information.

69 To avoid a snap hook, squeeze tightly with your right ring finger and "reach for the sky" on your follow-through.

70 There are two common errors that are major stumbling blocks that neophyte golfers must overcome.

First, every new golfer will swing through the ball with the back of the left hand facing skyward. Instead, their arms should "crossover" at impact so the left *palm* is facing nearly skyward on the finish. Second, every new golfer will "chop" down with the upper body rather than leading the forward swing with a hip turn to the target. Once these two common errors are corrected, a beginner will experience a dramatic improvement in scoring.

71 Your forearms should stay close together during the entire swing.

At address, your medial (inside) triceps should be tight against your rib cage.

72 **The right knee should not move at all on the backswing.**

Any movement of the right knee reduces the coiled power of the upper body and may destroy the correct plane of the swing.

73 **From time to time golfers using rubber grips should scrub them with soapy steel wool and dry them off with a rough towel.**

This revitalizes the optimum tackiness of the grips.

74 **Old golf balls putt funny.**

Cold golf balls don't go far.

Wet golf balls don't spin.

Range balls are club property.

75 **Take less club when playing from the rough, since the ball will usually roll when it lands.**

If there is a chance of leaving the ball in the rough, use a lofted club and get back on the fairway.

76 **When someone asks you what you shot, be unique.**

Just say a number and nothing more. Nobody wants to hear your sob stories. They only want to know if they beat you.

77 **If you must play golf on a rainy day, six things in your golf bag will make your day easier.**

- A zippered club cover should be secured at all times.

- A large, high-quality umbrella can also serve as a hanger for extra gloves and a dry towel.

- A water repellent rain suit that breathes will keep you warm, dry, and help prevent muscle cramps and strains.

- A broad-brimmed, bucket-style hat will keep water from running down your neck.

- Dry socks and a dry shirt are a morale booster at the turn. A cashmere sweater repels water.

- Granola-type bars eaten throughout a round will help maintain mental and physical energy.

  Note: Jack Nicklaus was renowned for seeing rain as an *opportunity* to overcome his adversaries.

78 If you take the game seriously, keep a USGA rule book in your bag and become proficient at using it for quick access during a round.

79 Playing with pros or low-handicap golfers will tend to elevate you to a higher level of play.

Good golf is infectious.

80 Concentration is the lack of conscious thought.

Calm your mind down, and let your "automatic pilot" hit the shot.

81 Think target.

On full shots and greenside, your thoughts should be focused *on your target* even though you are looking at your ball during the shot. For instance, if you had to toss a golf ball underhand to someone, your thoughts would not be on how far you swung your arm back or on how you gripped the ball. Your attention would be focused on the person's waiting hand. Once you are ready to execute the shot, keep the target in mind.

82 **If a certain hole consistently gives you fits, make a dramatic change in how you play it.**

If you seem to always pull your drive out of bounds, pick a radically different target off the tee or tee off using a 3 wood. If you always miss the green on your second shot, try a punch shot or force a shorter iron with a hard swing. Do something slightly different to break the pattern of failure.

83 **Beginners often hit many shots "thin."**

They don't get the club's leading edge under the ball. After many years of teaching, I made a startling discovery. While demonstrating an iron shot on a lush practice tee a student gasped as I properly took a healthy divot. She said, "Look what you did to the lawn!" I then realized the beginners, out of respect for manicured turf, flinch on shots to avoid taking a divot. Divots may be taboo on your front lawn, but they are *necessary* in hitting a solid iron shot.

84 A professional golfer's swing takes about one-and-a-half seconds from takeaway to follow-through.

An amateur golfer may swing in as little as half a second. A slow, full-shoulder turn and an extended follow-through not only take more time but also generate more clubhead speed. If you have trouble swinging "slow," try swinging "easy." It's almost the same thing.

85 When a professional shoots a round of 72, he might use his driver, sand iron, and putter as many as 52 times: 14 drives, 8 shots from around the green and in bunkers with a sand iron, and 30 putts.

Even an 18 handicapper often uses those three clubs for the majority of shots. They should be chosen carefully and remain your friends for years.

86 Many golfers ruin their score because they can't effectively play from bunkers.

A lesson in sand play technique followed by eight hours of work in a practice bunker will usually eliminate this obstacle.

87 To better execute a sand shot, tee up a ball in the bunker with the tee pushed fully down in the sand.

Then try to cut the tee in half with the leading edge of the sand wedge. By making "breaking the tee" your objective, you not only hit under the ball, but you will also swing with the force necessary to execute an "explosion" shot.

88 Hitting too closely to the ball on bunker shots will make the ball travel farther in the air and stop quicker.

Hitting too far behind the ball will shorten its flight and increase its roll. Both shots—struck with the same clubhead speed—will cause a ball to travel roughly the same distance; therefore, on sand shots, be more concerned with your clubhead's speed than with your striking distance behind the ball.

89 If you need to hit an intentional hook, here's a three-step process:

- aim at a secondary target to the right of your primary target

- grip your club with the face closed 20 or so degrees
- make your normal swing toward your secondary target

  With practice, you will learn exactly how much to shut the clubface for each shot.

90 **In match play, when your opponent is in trouble and a bogey will win the hole, don't take unnecessary risks.**

Readjust your strategy for that hole so you are sure to walk to the next tee with a win.

91 **When you arrive at the site of a tournament, seek out the host professional and spend a few minutes asking him for things to be aware of on his course.**

He will usually be more than happy to give you the benefit of his hard-earned local knowledge. It may be the difference between going home with a trophy and having "what if" memories.

92 If you've "lost your swing," play a carefree practice round in which you take only one look at the target and then pull the trigger.

You will be hitting shots by instinct and find your swing.

93 On side wind shots, it might be easier to ride the wind than to fight the wind.

Reserve the option to aim for a secondary target, playing the wind for a ride to the hole.

94 Play *real* golf once in a while.

Modern-day amateur golf usually allows for "picking up when out of the hole" and "taking a 7X." That is often accepted, but every golfer should play "strict rules" medal play once in a while. It may be painful to count every shot and have to put down an 11 on a hole, but that's the way real golf is played. You don't want to get out of the habit and forget how to score when you're in a situation where you must count every shot.

95 **If you are serious about lowering your score, keep a journal and record the little swing "keys" or thoughts or discoveries you used during a good round.**

You might think you'll never forget your discoveries, but six months later you may find yourself wondering how you played so well. Record your play in great detail so you can recreate what you did.

96 **After each round, assess your play on driving, iron shots, chipping, pitching, sand play, and putting.**

Also review your round for tactical errors. Is there a consistent area of underperformance? Always find the weakest link in your golf game and then work on eliminating it.

97 **Effective putting might be the most ephemeral facet of golf.**

Perhaps the single most common reason for putting poorly is focusing on what the putterhead is doing during the stroke. Instead, focus on stroking toward the hole. Be *target* conscious. Once you are aligned and ready to

putt, you should be able to raise your left arm
and point at the hole without taking your
eyes off the ball.

98 If you run a putt past the hole, watch how it breaks *beyond* the hole.

The ball will follow an almost identical line
back to the cup on your next putt.

99 For great putting pay attention to the grass.

If a putting surface looks a deeper green
than usual, you're probably putting into the
grain. If a green looks shiny and dry, you're
probably putting down grain. Putting with
the grain is a factor in the speed of the putt.
Going with the grain speeds the ball up;
against the grain slows it down. On Bermuda
grass and some other species, the grass will
dry out and turn brown on the down-grain
side of the cup as the exposed roots dry out
during the day.

100 Equipment may change, the rules of golf may change, but one thing remains: Golf is that rare game where the player is the primary umpire as well as the competitor.

Everyone who picks up a club either helps preserve the tradition and honor of the game—or contributes to its downfall.

101 What better place to enjoy God's creation than on a beautifully designed golf course?

Keeping that thought in mind may keep those 3-putt greens, out-of-bounds tee shots, bad lies, and fat iron shots in perspective. Golf is a tough game that can pull all sorts of emotions from us we didn't know were inside us. I am reminded of a framed cartoon in my dad's study. It showed a golfer with a bewildered look on his face standing by a tree, around which he had just wrapped one of his clubs. The caption read, "Ordinarily I'm such a *nice* guy!" That's golf!

Rick Graves has been a member of the PGA of America since 1973. He played the Asian Tour and other pro events before becoming a teaching professional. He taught at the first six PGA National Academy of Golf schools, authored golf's first yardage book, *Golf Log*, and ran a successful golf club in Vero Beach, Florida for 18 years. Whether playing or teaching the game he loves, Graves maintains a reputation for making golf instruction simple and successful.

Terry Glaspey has degrees in history and pastoral ministry and is the author of several books, including *Not a Tame Lion: The Spiritual Legacy of C.S. Lewis* and *Pathway to the Heart of God*. He is a passionate student of the Bible and a popular speaker for conferences and churches throughout North America. He loves golf, although he knows he should keep his day job.